KAUSHIK MADAPATI

Flutter Development for Gen. Z

Copyright © 2022 by Kaushik Madapati

All rights reserved. No part of this publication may be reproduced, stored or transmitted in any form or by any means, electronic, mechanical, photocopying, recording, scanning, or otherwise without written permission from the publisher. It is illegal to copy this book, post it to a website, or distribute it by any other means without permission.

Kaushik Madapati asserts the moral right to be identified as the author of this work.

Kaushik Madapati has no responsibility for the persistence or accuracy of URLs for external or third-party Internet Websites referred to in this publication and does not guarantee that any content on such Websites is, or will remain, accurate or appropriate.

First edition

This book was professionally typeset on Reedsy.
Find out more at reedsy.com

Contents

Acknowledgement		iv
1	Introduction	1
2	Why Flutter	4
3	Let's Get Flutter Installed!	9
4	Setting Up Our Development Environment!	21
5	Basic Syntax in Dart	29
6	Flutter Code Explained and Learning Our First Widgets!	40
7	Stateless and Stateful Widgets	61
8	What are Classes and Functions in Dart?	75
9	Understanding and Implementing Error Handling!	85
10	Let's Deploy Our App to the Public!	102
11	Conclusion	111
Glossary		112
About the Author		114

Acknowledgement

Thank you to all of my friends and family who have supported me in my development journey up to this point. None of this would have been possible without all of you.

1

Introduction

Have you ever wanted to build a mobile app? Well, for those with experience in native development, you almost definitely understand the struggles of developing the same app 3 times to fit three different platforms: iOS, Android, and web. After a certain point, you may have considered switching to cross-platform technologies as they have recently become popular among developer communities. The two most notable are Flutter and React Native, developed by Google and Facebook (which has now been renamed, Meta). However, you might not have switched, fearing a steep learning curve or having to relive all pain you went through to get to where you are now with this new technology. Or you could have thought that you were too late to learn it, and now you should just stick to what you are good or decent at. However, that might just be me.

You might wonder how I know all this because if the title is true, I am a member of the current generation and a young one, so what could I know about mobile development? I understand enough to have experienced these feelings and thoughts before. Now by no means am I saying that I am a professional developer, but I do have enough experience with iOS and Android development to understand the struggle of maintaining various code bases. And that only applies to apps that haven't yet been released to the public. Once on the App Store or the Google Play Store, it becomes a whole other ball game as minor bugs keep popping up, and it is very important to maintain the satisfaction of your users for your app to be considered worthwhile to the public. Furthermore, I have achieved awards for apps that I have created. Although these were apps made by high school and middle school kids, it shows that I understand app design basics. Everything I mentioned above ties back to the idea that the more steps involved in developing something, there are more places where something can go wrong. To solve this, I decided to learn Flutter (for reasons that I will cover later in this book) and document my journey in the form of this book. Throughout this book, I strive to explain the concepts in a way that a normal person could understand or, in other words, explain them at a very basic level. I am doing this because I understand the feeling of wanting to learn something new and instantly getting overwhelmed with complex ideas explained in ways that sounds like they were meant for college computer science students.

This book is a great starting point for those with no prior experience with mobile development or just development in general. This is because before diving into the Flutter-specific ideas, I will be going over the fundamentals of Dart (the language which Flutter is built upon), allowing you to wet your feet before we jump into the pool that is Flutter. Flutter is a great place to start your development journey, but you must understand the basics of programming first, and there are some Dart-specific things that should also be understood to make learning Flutter easier.

Finally, this book was written to introduce and familiarize the reader with the concepts in Flutter, meaning that there are no projects we will be developing together in this book. Rather I will take the time to explain each concept in detail, provide relevant examples, and showcase that concept's implementation if applicable. While I agree that the best way to learn is by doing, I also know that focusing too much on full projects when the fundamentals of the framework or language in question are not fully understood is a very easy way to build "false skills" which is something you want to avoid. This is also referred to as "getting stuck in tutorial land" where your skills depend entirely on your ability to follow and copy tutorials without completely understanding them. To avoid this, I have made this book more focused on the concepts and their individual implementations rather than their grouped implementations as a part of a larger project. However, this does not mean that this book has no projects. In fact, during the second half of the book most of the concepts I will explain will relate to 1 app. However, since this app is very simple, you will still understand the individual concepts. Furthermore, since Flutter is based around Dart (the language used in Flutter), many chapters in this book will cover Dart programming techniques and concepts. However, this does not mean that we won't be covering any Flutter concepts. We will be covering quite a few. At the end of the book, once you understand the entirety of the concepts covered, there will be a few projects to follow along with. Now, without further ado, let me start this book by explaining why I chose Flutter to base this book on instead of other tools.

2

Why Flutter

So why choose Flutter? This is a question that I can imagine being asked by several developers reading this book, specifically those who are well experienced with other cross-platform technologies such as React Native or even developers used to native development.

Before I can answer this question, I need to explain what Flutter is as a whole. Flutter is a cross-platform development framework developed by Google and initially launched in May 2017 that is built on Dart, a programming language created by Google. Furthermore, Flutter was made to integrate very quickly with several of Google's tools, such as Firebase, a database, and an authentication system. Flutter also makes it easy to integrate a back-end system built on Go, another programming language developed by Google. Starting to see the connections between all the tools? From my point of view, it seems an awful lot like Google is trying to build an entire development suite with authentication and database services, a front-end framework created on their own language, all of which integrate seamlessly with a language used for back-end development which they all happened to have developed. This promotes all their tools and makes the end-to-end process of developing an app much easier because all the tools required are provided by Google and, therefore, work well with each other.

Before I go any further, I must address a few things for the newer developers reading this book. I promised that I would explain the concepts covered in the simplest manner possible, including explaining these terms to newer developers. However, this may slowly become more and more tedious throughout this book. Therefore, at the back of this book, I have included a sort of "vocab list" for all the key terms I will use. More terms will appear throughout this book, but I will define those as we go along.

So, coming back to the main question of why choose Flutter? Compared to native development, Flutter is much more convenient because it does not require knowledge of several languages to work for several platforms, but it is also much easier to maintain because there is only one code base (a collection of all the code used). Furthermore, even while using native development, it is very difficult to make the app appear the same on all screen sizes. Flutter makes this much easier and, therefore, decreases development time. However, this doesn't mean that cross-platform technologies are going to replace native developers entirely. At least not for a long time because these technologies still have several limitations. Not only is the app bigger when released, but native apps also tend to perform better than cross-platform apps. Although, building an entire platform for several operating systems using native development is more time-consuming and also much more costly. For developers with a limited time frame and/or a limited budget, cross-platform development is the way to go. This is why I decided to focus on cross-platform development for this book.

Now all of that might already make sense to most cross-platform developers and even some native developers, but why am I using Flutter instead of other cross-platform technologies? Well, to answer that question, I first need to talk about the other cross-platform technologies. There are several technologies out there, but the most common competitor to Flutter is React Native, which is the tool I will use for this comparison.

Firstly, let's talk about their performance. Flutter's performance is higher than React Native's because, unlike React Native, Flutter compiles the entire app using the arm C/C++ library. Because of this, it becomes closer to a machine language, causing it to perform better on native platforms. However, React Native compiles the UI components to their native equivalents. This requires a javascript (often abbreviated as JS) bridge running in a separate thread to interact with the native elements. As a result, React Native's performance is worse than Flutter's.

On the topic of UI components, Flutter comes with several comprehensive UI components called widgets. However, React Native comes with very few UI components (which is what React Native calls them), making developers rely on third-party libraries to gain access to the UI components they want to use. This greatly increases development time and makes React Native harder to start with. Also, since Flutter keeps its widgets separate from the native versions, it helps prevent errors whenever new updates are pushed. The same cannot be said about React Native, however. However, this doesn't mean the widgets in Flutter are purely superior to UI components in React Native. One major downside with widgets in Flutter is that they need to be configured manually, whereas some components in React Native are adaptive (meaning that they adapt to the layout of the device) automatically. As of whatever time you are reading this, things might have changed if Flutter was recently updated with new features.

Furthermore, the languages that these frameworks use are different, which is where React Native starts to shine more. Flutter uses Dart, which is an object-oriented programming language built by Google and launched in October of 2011, whereas React Native uses Javascript, which is a very common programming language that several developers already have experience with. Javascript is a language commonly used to add functionality to web pages and is paired with several frameworks/libraries to create the back-end of a web app. One of these frameworks is React, which is not to be confused with React Native. React is a library paired with Javascript to create UI components for web apps, whereas React Native is a cross-platform framework used to create apps that work on iOS, Android, and the web. However, the syntax and methods used are very similar. React is a very popular tool used with Javascript. Many developers already have experience with it, making React Native much easier to pick up. However, Dart isn't all bad. Dart's syntax is very similar to that of Java and Javascript and is an extremely high-performing programming language, meaning it compiles faster than Javascript. Finally, Flutter apps are smooth and run a 60 FPS (frames per second), which is much better than the performance of React Native.

Finally, we need to discuss Flutter and React Native's statuses in the industry currently. React Native has been around for 2 years more than Flutter, meaning that its adoption rate by larger companies is higher than Flutter. This means that there are more resources to learn about React Native than Flutter, and since it has been in development longer, it would make sense that React Native would be more stable in some cases. Now, this does not mean that Flutter is impossible to learn and/or is very unstable. The latest version of Flutter (as of the time this book is being written), Flutter 3, is stable for all platforms. Google has put a lot of effort into making the Flutter releases as stable as possible and the Flutter developer community is growing rapidly. However, the fact that React Native is more mature than Flutter is indisputable.

After reading all of this, you may have your own opinion on which cross-platform framework based on what you look for in a framework. Some prioritize performance and ease of use out of the box, while others prioritize how easy it is for them to learn, which steers many people towards React Native since many developers already have experience in Javascript. However, as this book is more centered on explaining concepts on a simpler level, it makes it easier to start with Flutter because it comes with several widgets. Furthermore, not only does Flutter perform better than React Native, but both Flutter and Dart are rapidly growing; therefore, learning it earlier may prove beneficial down the line.

3

Let's Get Flutter Installed!

Now that you understand what Flutter is and why we are using it, we next need to get it installed and properly set up. However, the steps differ for macOS, Windows, and Linux (Chrome OS is not covered in this book). For this reason, this portion of the chapter will be split into 3 parts to accommodate the different operating systems, so feel free to skip ahead to the section that pertains to your computer's operating system, but if you choose to look through the other sections, you will find that the content for some operating systems is pretty much verbatim to the other. This is the case for macOS and Linux because macOS is built on Linux. If you happen to encounter any errors while installing Flutter that I did not cover, I would recommend either searching online or heading over to "https://docs.flutter.dev/get-started/install" and seeing if your error was addressed in their installation documentation. Finally, before we start installing Flutter, I recommend creating a folder on your desktop titled "Flutter" because I will be referencing that folder in the following commands and it also makes it easier to have all the flutter files and all of your projects stored in one folder.

However, if you decide not to create a Flutter folder on your desktop, then you will need to change your path accordingly in any steps that may require you to input your path.

Installation for macOS

Firstly, it is recommended that you have Xcode installed, and this is because in order to install and update Flutter, you need to have Git installed, and Git is included in Xcode. If you do not have Git installed, open your terminal and run the following command:

```
brew install git
```

If you are getting an error mentioning a permissions issue, then add "sudo" in front of the above command and enter your password when prompted. This fixes the error in most cases.

However, if you are getting an error that says brew is not a recognized command, then you do not have Homebrew installed, which is what the brew command is referencing. You can download Homebrew by typing the following command in your terminal (for this command and all commands that have multiple lines, unless they are separate commands, do not create an extra line when typing the command, just continue the command on the same line):

```
/bin/bash -c "$(curl -fsSL
https://raw.githubusercontent.com/Homebrew/
install/HEAD/install.sh)"
```

This command is very long and can be very annoying to copy down from a book and type into a terminal. Instead of doing this, you can just visit "https://brew.sh/" and copy the command under the heading that reads, "Install Homebrew" and paste it into your terminal.

After this, Git should be installed, and we can begin installing Flutter.

Now that all the preparations are complete ensure that you have 2.8 GB of storage available on your computer. Note that this does not include space for your IDE and/or other tools. If you use a newer Mac with an Apple Silicon chip, make sure to run the following command in your terminal before proceeding with the installation.

```
sudo softwareupdate --install-rosetta
--agree-to-license
```

Next, navigate to "https://docs.flutter.dev/get-started/install/macos" and scroll down to the section that reads "Get the Flutter SDK" (the Flutter SDK is just all the files that Flutter needs to run). Below, click the blue button under the text that best describes your computer's CPU: either Intel or Apple Silicon. As you scroll down through this site, you might question why I am typing out the commands here if I could just have you visit this site and copy everything from there. I am doing it this way because the website does not cover all the installation steps in detail, and many things can go wrong, leading to several errors. For that reason, in this chapter, I will cover the common errors and the solutions to them that can occur during Flutter installation.

Once the zip file containing the Flutter SDK has been downloaded and stored in your Downloads folder, run the following commands:

```
cd Desktop/Flutter/
unzip ~/Downloads/flutter_macos_3.0.2-stable.zip
```

The last portion of the 2nd command will change based on what the file name of the zip is for the Flutter SDK. For the current version, when it is downloaded, it is named "flutter_macos_3.0.2-stable.zip" assuming the same zip file does not already exist on your computer. Now Flutter is installed on your computer. Let's try running a command! Run the following command in your already open terminal window:

```
flutter doctor
```

Unless you already have Flutter set up, you will get an error saying that "flutter" is not a recognized command. How do we fix this? We fix this by running the following command, which adds the "flutter" tool to our path, allowing us to use the "flutter" command. Run the following command:

```
export PATH="$PATH:`pwd`/flutter/bin"
```

Now if you run the "flutter doctor" command again you will start to see that it works and you will see a lot of terminal output that we will decipher together. However, we need to tidy something up first. The command listed above only allows us to use the "flutter" command in the current terminal instance, and while this could work, it can get tedious to have to either run this command every single time you open your terminal or keep a single terminal window open at all times which could close in case your computer runs out of battery or unexpectedly crashes. So we will have to update the path so we can always use the "flutter" command in our terminal window. Firstly run the following command in your terminal window:

```
echo $SHELL
```

If the output contains "zsh", you are using the Z shell; if the output contains "bash", then you are using Bash. No matter what shell you are using, you need to edit a specific file within that shell. To do that, run the following command:

```
echo "export PATH=$PATH:/Users/[current user profile]/Desktop/Flutter/flutter/bin" >> ~/.zshrc
```

The command will work perfectly if you are using Z Shell. However, if you are using Bash, you need to replace the "~/.zshrc" with "~./bashrc" and it should work.

To verify that everything is working fine, close the current terminal window, open a new terminal window, and run the following commands:

```
echo $PATH
which flutter
```

If, for both commands you get a path as an output, then you have successfully gained access to the "flutter" command meaning that you can use it in several different terminal windows on your computer without needing to run any prior commands.

Now we can proceed with the installation, and there is only 1 major step left: to ensure that all the necessary tools are installed on your computer to run Flutter. Run the following command in your terminal (note that this command does not need to be run in the Flutter folder, but I would still recommend running all Flutter-related commands in your Flutter folder):

```
flutter doctor
```

If the output at the bottom reads "No Issues Found!" you are ready to go, and you can skip the next chapter (although I recommend you read through it) because everything needed is already present on your computer. If you are not getting the above messages, one or more things are not installed on your computer. You can ignore these messages for now and skip ahead to the next chapter, where we will set up our development environment and fix these issues, but I would recommend installing Xcode if you haven't already just because it allows you to test the apps on an iOS simulator however it is by no means required as we will be testing our code on an Android simulator for this book.

Installation for Linux

Before installing Flutter on your Linux system, please ensure that your operating system is 64-bit and that your computer has at least 600 MB of storage available for installing Flutter. Please note that this does not include the extra disk space required for your IDE and/or other tools. Furthermore, please confirm that you have the following command-line tools available in your environment:

```
bash
curl
file
git 2.[version number]
mkdir
rm
unzip
which
xz-utils
zip
libGLU.so.1 (provided by mesa packages with different
commands for different versions of Linux to be able
to run "flutter test")
```

If any of the above command-line tools are not already installed on your computer, please download them as they are required to install and set up Flutter successfully. Once you have confirmed that your computer satisfies all the prerequisites above, you can begin installing Flutter.

Firstly, navigate to "https://docs.flutter.dev/get-started/install/linux" and scroll down to the section "Install Flutter manually". You are free to install Flutter using snapd if you wish, but I am going through the manual installation in this book because I want to demonstrate some key ideas that are not demonstrated when you install Flutter through snapd. As you scroll down through this site, you might find that most of what is on this website is what I am covering in this chapter, and you may be tempted to follow the website instead of this guide. You are free to do so, but I highly recommend following my explanation as I will go through common errors and how to fix them. Next, click the blue button that should be a ".tar.xz" file with the latest Flutter release.

Once the zip file containing the Flutter SDK has been downloaded and stored in your Downloads folder, run the following commands:

```
cd Desktop/Flutter/
tar xf ~/Downloads/flutter_linux_3.0.2-stable.zip
```

The last portion of the 2nd command will change based on what the file name of the zip is for the Flutter SDK. For the current version, when it is downloaded, it is named "flutter_linux_3.0.2-stable.zip" assuming the same ".tar.xz" file does not already exist on your computer. Now Flutter is installed on your computer. Let's try running a command! Run the following command in your already open terminal window:

```
flutter doctor
```

Unless you already have Flutter set up, you will get an error saying that "flutter" is not a recognized command. How do we fix this? We fix this by running the following command, which adds the "flutter" tool to our path, allowing us to use the "flutter" command. Run the following command:

```
export PATH="$PATH:`pwd`/flutter/bin"
```

Now, if you run the "flutter doctor" command again, you will start to see that it works and a lot of terminal output that we will decipher together. However, we need to tidy something up first. The command listed above only allows us to use the "flutter" command in the current terminal instance, and while this could work, it can get tedious to have to either run this command every single time you open your terminal or keep a single terminal window open at all times which could close in case your computer runs out of battery or unexpectedly crashes. So we will have to update the path so we can always use the "flutter" command in our terminal window. To do this, you must open your file explorer and go to the home folder. Press the "Ctrl" key and the "h" key at the same time to view hidden files and look for a file named ".bashrc". Once you find that file, open it and add the following line to the bottom of that file:

```
export PATH="$PATH:/home/[current user profile]/Desktop/Flutter/flutter/bin"
```

If you do not see that file, you must create it and add the above command. Once you do that, save the file and close it. To verify that everything is working fine, close the current terminal window, open a new terminal window, and run the following commands:

```
echo $PATH
which flutter
```

If, for both commands, you get a path as an output, then you have successfully gained access to the "flutter" command meaning that you can use it in several different terminal windows on your computer without needing to run any prior commands.

Now we can proceed with the installation, and there is only 1 major step left: to ensure that all the necessary tools are installed on your computer to run Flutter. Run the following command in your terminal (note that this command does not need to be run in the Flutter folder, but I would still recommend running all Flutter-related commands in your Flutter folder):

```
flutter doctor
```

If the output at the bottom reads "No Issues Found!" you are ready to go, and you can skip the next chapter (although I recommend you read through it) because everything needed is already present on your computer. If you are not getting the above messages, one or more things are not installed on your computer. You can ignore these messages for now and skip to the next chapter, where we will set up our development environment and fix these issues.

Installation for Windows

Before we begin installing Flutter, ensure that your computer is running Windows 10 or later (64-bit), x86-64 based. Furthermore, make sure you have 1.64 GB of storage available to install Flutter. Note that this does not include extra storage required for installing an IDE and/or other tools. Also, make sure that you have Git 2.[version number] installed. If you do not have Git installed, navigate to the following website:

```
https://git-scm.com/download/win
```

Once on that website, select the "64-bit GIT for Windows Setup" option and install Git.

Once you have installed Git, you are ready to install Flutter. Navigate to "https://docs.flutter.dev/get-started/install/windows" and scroll down to the section that reads "Get the Flutter SDK" and click the blue button below step 1. As you scroll down through this site, you might question why I am typing out the commands here if I could just have you visit this site and copy everything from there. I am doing it this way because the website does not cover all the installation steps in detail, and many things can go wrong, leading to several errors. For that reason, in this chapter, I will cover the common errors and the solutions to them that can occur during Flutter installation.

Once you have downloaded the zip file, extract it and place the contained "flutter" folder in the Flutter folder on your desktop (or in whatever place you wish to install Flutter). Now Flutter is installed on your computer. Let's try running a command! Open a new Powershell window and run the following command:

```
flutter doctor
```

Unless you already have Flutter set up, you will get an error saying that "flutter" is not a recognized command. How do we fix this? We fix this by running the following command, which adds the "flutter" tool to our path, allowing us to use the "flutter" command. To do this, go to your Start search bar and enter "env". Then, select "Edit the system environment variables". Then, click on the button that reads "Environment Variables" at the bottom. If there is a user variable that is named "Path", double-click it and check if there is a path that reads "C:/Users/[current user]/Desktop/Flutter/flutter/bin". If there is, you are all set up and can move on ahead. If there is no path that reads that, then you have to select the new icon and add the above path. If there is no user variable named "Path" for you, then you need to click new, type in "Path" and follow the step above. Once that is done, you can press "Okay" at the bottom of the window and close all the other windows relating to environment variables. Once that is done, all we need to do is ensure that all the necessary tools are installed on your computer to run Flutter. To do that, run the following command in your terminal (note that this command does not need to be run in the Flutter folder, but I would still recommend running all Flutter-related commands in your Flutter folder):

```
flutter doctor
```

If the output at the bottom reads "No Issues Found!" you are ready to go, and you can skip the next chapter (although I still recommend you read through it) because everything needed is already on your computer. If you are not getting the above messages, one or more things are not installed on your computer. You can ignore these messages now and skip to the next chapter, where we will set up our development environment and fix these issues.

4

Setting Up Our Development Environment!

Now that we have Flutter installed and set up, we need to set up our development environment. We need to install an IDE or an integrated development environment to do this. An IDE is an app (or website in the case of sites like replit.com) where you can write code. There are many different IDEs that we can use for Flutter, so in this chapter, I will be talking about the different IDEs that we can use and which one I highly recommend using when developing apps with Flutter.

So what are the IDEs that can be used to develop with Flutter? The 3 main ones are IntelliJ Idea, Visual Studio Code, and Android Studio. However, I think the main competition is between Visual Studio Code and Android Studio because Android Studio is built on the same platform, IntelliJ Idea, so they are very similar. Visual Studio Code is much more lightweight than Android Studio and allows for much more versatility because of how many extensions it supports. This does not mean that Android Studio is not versatile. However, it is less versatile and better known for developing Android apps. However, it does support Flutter as an extension and its seamless integration with simulators makes it the ideal choice, in my opinion, for development with Flutter. Therefore, in this chapter, we are going to be setting up Android Studio to develop with Flutter, and this directly ties back to the output result you got back from Flutter when you ran "flutter doctor". You can ignore the portion of Visual Studio Code in the output because that is not required and the error regarding the "connected device" or the simulator because we will fix that later in this chapter. The most important thing, for now, is to make the message that reads "Flutter (Channel stable)" checked off because that means that Flutter has been installed safely on your computer. I would also recommend using Chrome if you plan to deploy apps to the web. Most of you will probably get a message like the following when you run "flutter doctor":

```
[-] Android toolchain - develop for Android devices
 Android SDK at /Users/[current
 user]/Library/Android/sdk✗
  Android SDK is missing command line tools; download
  from https://goo.gl/XxQghQ
 Try re-installing or updating your Android SDK,
 visit https://docs.flutter.dev/setup/#android-setup
 for detailed instructions.
```

Note that the message might be slightly different depending on your operating system. Let's start fixing these errors. If you haven't already, download Android Studio from "https://developer.android.com/studio". Once you have downloaded it, open it, and your screen should look something like this:

SETTING UP OUR DEVELOPMENT ENVIRONMENT!

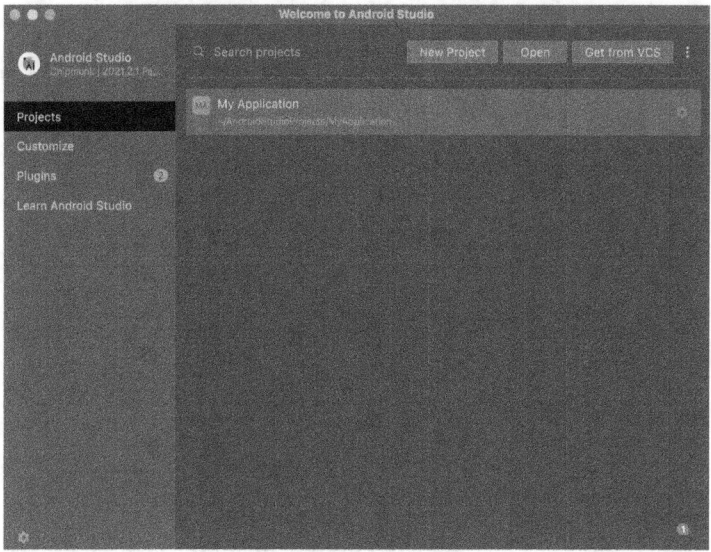

Depending on your operating system, it may look a little different, but the layout should be generally the same. If you do not see the 3 vertical dots, you may have to click "More Actions" to find the options list. Before you do anything else, you want to click on "Plugins", search for Flutter, and install it. Then click on the projects tab to return to the screen you see above. Next, you want to click on the 3 vertical dots next to the button that reads "Get from VCS". Once you do that, select the "SDK Manager" option. Once you do that, you should be presented with a screen that looks like this:

From there, click on the "SDK Tools" bar and select all the boxes that I have checked below:

It is okay if some of these do not appear on your window. The main ones we need are "Android SDK Command-line Tools (latest)", "Android Emulator", "Android SDK Platform-Tools", and "Android SDK Build-Tools". Once you have selected the boxes, click "OK" at the bottom of the window, and a new window will pop up asking you to confirm the installation that will look something like this:

> ⚠ **Confirm Change**
> The following components will be installed:

At the bottom of the window, click "OK" and the installation of these tools will begin. Then another window will pop up with the installation progress. Once it is finished, click "Finish" at we have successfully installed the necessary tools needed from Android Studio. Next is addressing the simulator issue. If you are on a Mac, you may already have the Simulator app installed, allowing you to test your apps on Apple devices. For Mac users, you can open the Simulator app by running the following command in your terminal:

open -a Simulator

Once you run that command, an iPhone should appear on your screen and start to boot up. However, in this book, we will be using Android simulators just for ease of use across multiple operating systems. Firstly, we should check if we have any existing simulators that can be used with Flutter. We can determine this by running the command below:

```
flutter emulators
```

Once you run that command, a list should come up of all the emulators you can use. Some of you may already have an Android simulator already ready to use. If you see an Android simulator in the list when you run the above command, then run the following command:

```
flutter emulators --launch [device id which you can
directly copy and paste from the list above (the
device id is the name with underscores, for example,
Pixel_3a_API_30_x86)]
```

If you do not see any devices or get an error when running the command, you can continue to follow along with this chapter. However, if you were able to launch the simulator, you are good to go with your development environment, and you can skip to the next chapter. If you saw the simulator, ran the command, and got an error, it is likely that you are on an Apple Silicon-powered Mac. It doesn't work due to a condition in the simulator code that doesn't allow chips with Apple Silicon architecture to use simulators with an API level of 28 or higher. The condition is shown below:

```
#ifdef __x86_64__
    if (sarch == "arm64" && apiLevel >=28) {
        APANIC("Avd's CPU Architecture '%s' is not
        supported by the QEMU2 emulator on x86_64
        host.\n", avdarch);
    }
#endif
```

For this reason, we will be setting up a simulator with API level 27, so it satisfies the condition. If no simulators show up in your terminal when you run "flutter emulators", then you should follow along. The first thing you need to do is go back to the

Android Studio home page. Once you are there, click on the 3 vertical dots and select the option that says "Virtual Device Manager". Then you should see a window that looks like the following:

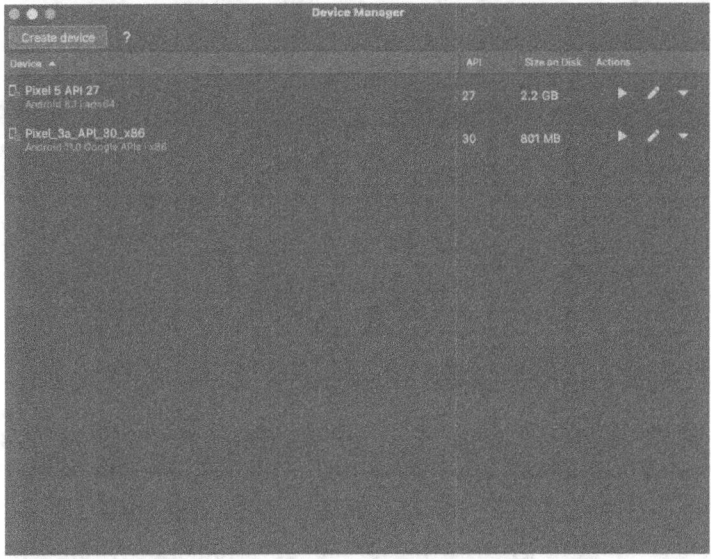

Keep in mind that my window looks different as I already have a few simulators. Next, you want to click on the "Create device" button. Once you click that button, you should see a screen with a list of devices. From there, I recommend selecting the Pixel 5 because that is the simulator we use in this book. However, it doesn't matter. Once you select your simulator, click the "Next" button and select the API level. I recommend using API level 27 if you are running on a Mac with an Apple Silicon chip because it is the newest API level you can use on an Android simulator. At this point, your screen should look like this:

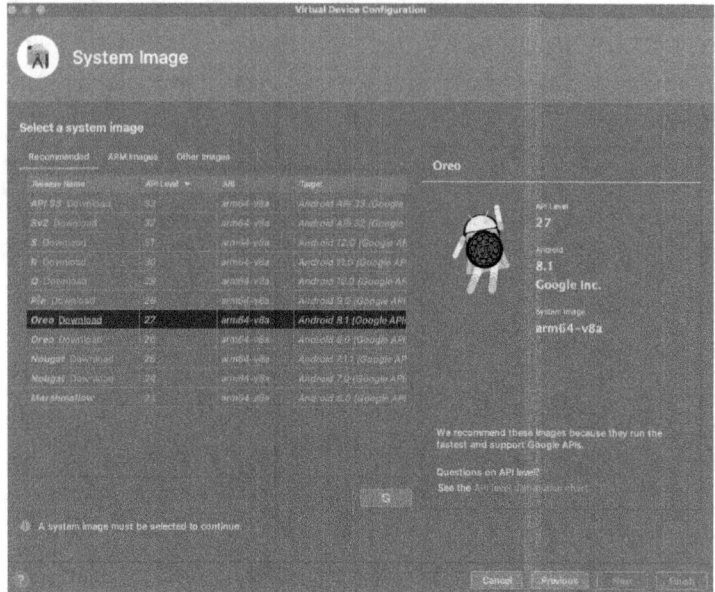

Then click on the blue button that says "Download" next to the API level and let it download, and click the button that says "Finish" when the installation is done. After that, you successfully finished setting up your development environment for Flutter!

5

Basic Syntax in Dart

Now that we have finished setting up our development environment for Flutter, we can start learning Flutter. The first thing we need to do is learn the language that Flutter depends on, Dart. Dart is a programming language built by Google which was launched in 2011. It has a syntax that has been called similar to Java and Javascript. Since we are just experimenting with Dart and not building a Flutter app in this chapter, we will use an online tool to write Dart code. This online tool is called replit.com and allows people to test code in multiple programming languages without downloading a specific IDE onto their computer. To access this tool, you must open a web browser and go to "replit.com"; if you do not have an account, you will need to create one. Once you have created an account, you will be sent to the home screen where we can create a file where all the Dart code we write in this chapter will be stored. Click on the blue button that says "Create" on the side menu, and a popup will appear asking you to enter the name of the repl (which is what replit calls their files) and the language you want to use for that file. In the language text box, type Dart, and for the file name, type whatever you want; however, I would highly recommend naming it something that you can find easily, such as "DartPractice". Once you have done that, click "Create Repl" and you will be navigated to a code editor with nothing but a function inside it that should look like this:

```dart
void main() {
   print('Hello World!');
}
```

So what is this function? Well, for those of you reading that have experience with Java, C++, or a few other languages, you will understand this function very well. This is because if you have any experience with those languages, you will almost definitely have used this function with every project you did. This function is called the main function, and it is called that because it is a very important function in our code. The main function is responsible for running all library functions and any statements or functions we create. Essentially, any Dart script requires the main function for its execution. The main function is now filled with nothing but a simple print statement. A print statement is a line of code used to output text or data of many forms to the console. A console in an IDE is a place where you can view the results of the commands in the script. For example, if you were to run this Dart script, you would get the following output.

BASIC SYNTAX IN DART

```dart
void main() {
  print('Hello World!');
}
```

```
> dart main.dart
Hello World!
>
```

The console can be used to view errors or messages that may later be displayed to the user via the UI (also known as the user interface) of the app. In many programming languages, every character matters, and a great example of this in Dart is the semicolon. The semicolon is a symbol used to indicate the end of a line of code, and without it, that line of code won't work.

```dart
void main() {
  print('Hello World!')
}
```

```
> dart main.dart
main.dart:2:23: Error: Expected ';' af
ter this.
  print('Hello World!')
                      ^
exit status 254
>
```

Now that we have gone over the main function, let's start creating some variables. Variables can be best understood as containers of data. In some programming languages, the type of data has to be explicitly mentioned when creating the variable. These types of data can be numbers (called integers or ints for short), characters (called strings), decimals (called floats or doubles depending on their size), or true or false values (called booleans or bools for short). These variables are called type-specific. These programming languages include Java, C++, C#, and more. In other programming languages, the type of data stored does not need to be specified, meaning that variables are empty containers for data with no preferences. Python is an example of a language that uses these types of variables. Then, we have languages like Dart, which allow you to use both type-specific variables and non-type-specific variables. However, there are advantages to each type of variable, which we will go into soon. The main focus of this chapter will be on 3 topics: variables, conditionals, and iteration. There are other important concepts such as classes and functions that are also a big part of Dart, but in my opinion, these concepts are best understood through experience, which is why we will have gone through quite a bit of Flutter development before we get to classes and functions in Dart. When we do eventually reach that portion, you will already understand the basic concept, which allows you to pick up their advanced uses much quicker.

Variables

As mentioned above, Dart allows us to use both type-specific and non-type-specific variables. However, this doesn't mean we should always use non-type-specific variables. For example, if we were using a function to add 2 numbers together and we did not specify the numbers as integers, then if we passed in 2 sentences, the computer would not know what to expect, and the outcome would not be what we desire. However, if we specified that the 2 variables we wanted to add had to be integers and we passed in 2 sentences, the computer could tell us that we were supposed to pass in numbers, not sentences. In general, I do recommend using type-specific variables as it makes debugging easier, and it is just a good programming practice so that if you ever were to use a language with type-specific variables, then it would not be difficult to adjust. However, I will start with non-type-specific variables because it flattens the learning curve for beginners to programming without experience with variables. With a non-type-specific variable, we do not need to specify the type of data that is being stored in that variable. That also means we can change the type of data stored anywhere in our code. An example of this is below:

```
dynamic cars;
cars = 12;
cars = false;
cars = 1.9;
cars = "Red Toyota";
```

As you can see, we are using the same variable to store data of several types, and if we were to call a print statement at the end of all of this code then the output would be "Red Toyota". As you can see in order to create a variable that does not conform to any specific type of data, we need to use the keyword "dynamic". This is one of the 3 main types of variables in Dart. We just talked about dynamic-type variables, inferred-type variables, and static-type variables. Static-type variables are the same as type-specific variables meaning that you need to specify the type of data being stored in the variable when you create it, and you are not allowed to store data of any other type in that variable. The type of data that can be stored in the variable is determined by a few keywords such as "int", "String", and "bool". A few examples are this are shown below:

```
String firstName = "Robert";
  int age = 25;
  bool isHuman = true;
```

Finally, we have inferred-type variables, which I view as a mix of static and dynamic-type variables. Inferred-type variables can only store 1 type of data. However, that type of data does not have to be specified when you create the variable. Rather, the type of data that can be stored in that variable is determined by the initial value stored in that variable. Two examples of this are shown below:

```
var random = 9.23;
var num = "Hello world!";
```

In the above examples, the "var" keyword specifies an inferred-type variable, and that type is determined by the value following it. This is shown when the variable random now has a type of float (relatively small decimal) because its initial value is a float value, and therefore, that is the type for the variable. Now you may be wondering what if you don't want to specify an initial value or if you want to create a variable that you couldn't change? To create a variable without specifying an initial value, you can always initialize it with null, which is equivalent to nothing. A few examples of this are shown below:

```
String name;
float decimal;
```

```
int numOfPets;
dynamic dogs;
```

With all of the variables above, they have no specified value, so in case you don't have a starting value to create the variable with, you can always create it with a null value. However, with inferred-type variables, if you specify them as a null value, they become a dynamic variable. If you don't want the type to change on an inferred-type variable, I suggest putting a placeholder value because otherwise, it will become a dynamic variable. But what if you don't want the value to change? Well, this brings us to the 2 other types of variables that don't fall under the main variables category, but they are definitely important to remember. These variables are constants and final variables. A constant variable is one that stays the same when compiled. Final variables are variables that, once defined, cannot be changed later in the code. An example of a constant variable and an example of a final variable has been shown below:

```
const speed = 20.45;
final name = "Bob";
```

Constant variables and final variables are also inferred-type variables, as you can see from the lack of specific keywords that describe the type of data that is being stored in that variable. Those 3 main types of variables: static-type variables, dynamic-type variables, and inferred-type variables, cover the main concepts that need to be understood about Dart regarding variables.

Conditionals

Now that you understand how to store data into containers called variables, you need to understand how to perform actions under certain conditions. This idea is commonly used in real life. For example, if it is hot, you turn on the AC, and otherwise, you leave the AC off. This idea is also greatly important in programming. In this conditionals section, we will be looking at if, else if, and else statements. There are also switch statements that are important. However, learning them is not necessary to understand just the fundamentals of Dart. If statements are pretty intuitive. The basic logic is: If this, then that. Going back to our AC example, an if statement for this case would be: If temperature > 85 degrees, turn on AC. The syntax for if statements in Dart is quite similar to what we just did above. This is an example of an if statement in Dart:

```
int age = 25;
if (age < 18) {
   print("You are not an adult");
}
```

As you can see, the syntax is pretty intuitive, and since 25 is not less than 18, it doesn't tell us that we are not adults. The curly braces represent the scope of this statement. This means that anything inside those 2 curly braces applies to that statement in particular and not the rest of the code. However, if we look back at the if statement, what is the user being told since they are older than 18? They aren't being told anything. To tell the user something, we need to add an else and/or an else if statement. Adding the else if and the else functionality is quite simple to do. The else statement is used if none of the above conditions are met, meaning it is the last resort. The else if statement is to add another condition to check before resorting to the else statement. An example of this is shown below:

```
String name = "Bob";
if (name == "John") {
  print("Your name is John");
} else if (name == "Bob") {
  print("Your name is Bob");
} else {
  print("Your name is not John or Bob");
}
```

As you can, the condition in the if statement doesn't prove to be correct, so it checks the else if, which is correct, meaning that we can run the code inside the else if statement, and we don't have to resort to the else statement. Note that I used a double equal sign to symbolize that those 2 values were equal. In Dart and many other programming languages, a single equal sign is used to assign values, whereas 2 equal signs are used to compare values. If you wanted to add one more condition in the if statement, then you could use the "or" operator, which is "||" or the "and" operator, which is "&&". If you use the "and" operator, all of the conditions in that statement must be evaluated to be true for the code inside that statement to run. However, if you use the "or" operator, only 1 of the values inside that condition must be true for the code inside that statement to run. With that, we have covered pretty much everything needed to understand the basics of conditionals in Dart.

Iteration

In this section of the chapter, we will be talking about 2 main ways to iterate through data in Dart and pretty much all programming languages: for loops and while loops. The main difference between a for loop and a while loop is that for loops operate on a condition with a variable created with the for loop, whereas while loops just operate on a condition in general. An example of a for loop is shown below:

```
int sum = 0;
for (int i = 0; i < 10; i++) {
    sum += i;
}
```

If you are unfamiliar with programming, it can be very easy to get lost with for loops, so I will try my best to break it down. Firstly, the purpose of this loop is to calculate the sum of all numbers from 0 to 10. So to do that, we create a variable called sum, which is initially equal to 0. Then we start the for loop. Before we start "looping", we need to initialize our index variable, as I call it. I call it an index variable because for loops are commonly used with lists which we will learn later in this book. But basically, this variable "i" that we are creating inside the for loop is going to serve as our counter, and we also have the ability to place limits on it, such as its max value. This max value also serves as the number of times that this loop can run in this case. The "i++" portion just means that "i" is increased by 1 with each loop. Finally, we have the line "sum += i". This is a shorthand for writing "sum = sum + i". For loops tend to seem daunting to beginners, which is why many tend to gravitate towards while loops. While loops operate on a condition similar to for loops (i < 10). However, while loops don't define their own variable and operate with a condition based on that variable. An example of a while loop is shown below:

```
int i = 1;
while (i < 10) {
    print(i);
    i++;
}
```

This looks much simpler than a for loop, which is why most beginners gravitate towards while loops. In this code segment, we are first creating a variable called "i" which is set to 1 initially. Then we create a while loop that continues looping as long as "i" is less than 10. Within this loop, we are printing the value of "i" and the final line "i++" is just a short way of writing "i = i + 1". Now that you understand the basics of variables, conditionals, and iteration in Dart, you are almost ready to learn Flutter-specific content. However, there are two more topics that we need to discuss first.

6

Flutter Code Explained and Learning Our First Widgets!

Now that you have a basic understanding of Dart, it is about time that we finally began learning Flutter. If you have successfully set up Android Studio for Flutter development, then when you open Android Studio, you should see a button that says "New Flutter Project" or something along those lines. The button will be on a screen like this:

FLUTTER CODE EXPLAINED AND LEARNING OUR FIRST WIDGETS!

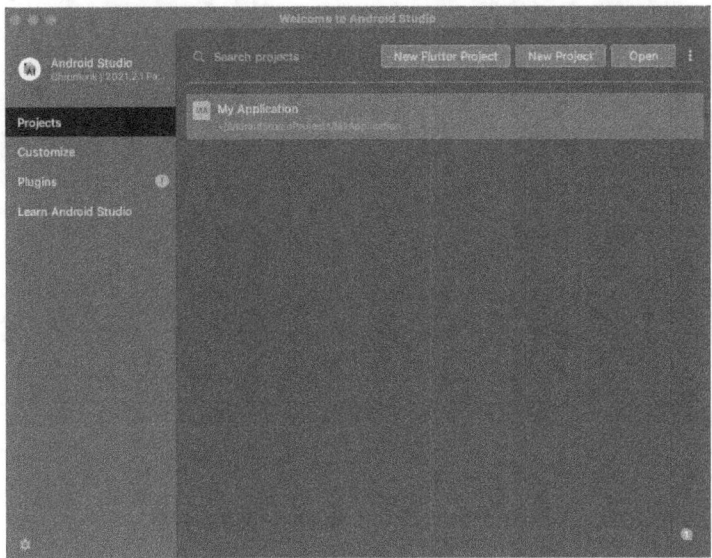

You can also find this option if you go to the top menu bar and click "File" and then "New". Once you do that, you should see an option to create a new Flutter project. No matter how you create the Flutter project, the important thing is that you create it. Feel free to title it whatever you wish. However, I would suggest naming it so you can find it again. For example, you could name it "first_flutter_app". Dart has a few requirements for creating names with projects, such as all lowercase and no spaces. When creating the project, Android Studio may ask for the location of your Flutter SDK, and there should be a Flutter option. Click on that option and allow Android Studio to access any necessary folders. Then select all the platforms under the section that asks what platforms you want your app to run on. Don't worry too much about the other settings; leave them as they are. Once created, you should see a screen like this:

This is the main.dart file where pretty much all of the code for our Flutter app is stored. Later we will discuss classes you can use to separate your code into multiple files. Now that we see our main.dart file, let's start breaking it down. Firstly, you should notice how it says "class MyApp extends Stateless Widget" and later in the file, it says "class MyHomePage extends Stateful Widget". We will cover what the "extend" keyword does in a later chapter when we discuss classes but what exactly are stateless and stateful widgets? Well, to answer that question, there are a few things that we need to go over first, as if we dive into stateless and stateful widgets without learning these things, it can become really easy to get lost. For that reason, in this chapter, we will focus on the general structure of Flutter code and common widgets before we cover stateless and stateful widgets in the next chapter.

Firstly, let's break down the overall organization of our Flutter app in Android Studio. Currently, this is the structure of our Flutter project:

FLUTTER CODE EXPLAINED AND LEARNING OUR FIRST WIDGETS!

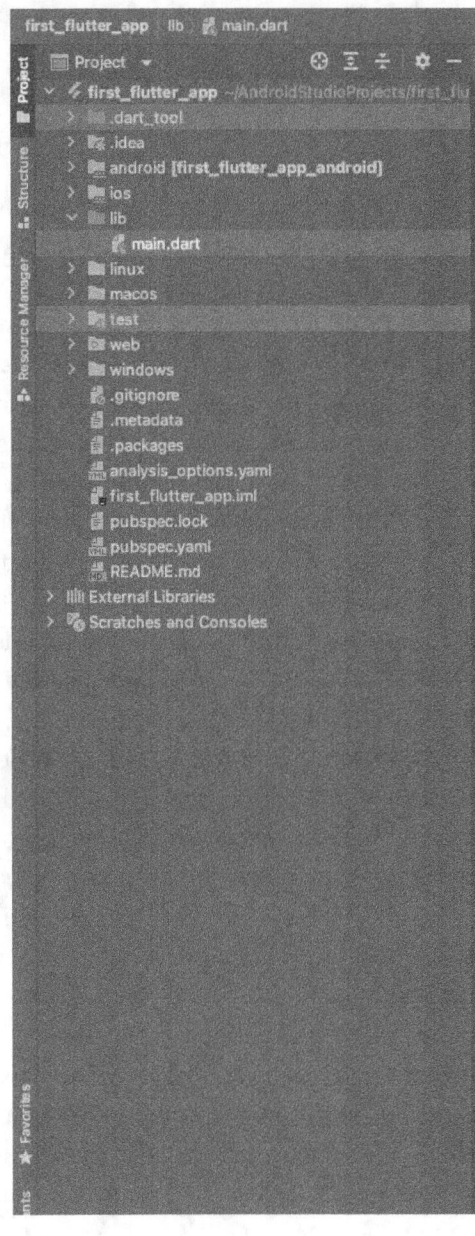

As you can see, there are several folders that may appear daunting to some, but in reality, it is quite simple. The different folders for the platforms, such as "macOS" and "Linux" are folders that contain platform-specific information. We won't be using those folders right now as they are mainly used for platform-specific data such as icons for devices on that platform. There is also an "External Libraries" folder which is where any libraries that we install that our app depends on are stored. The main focus, for now, should be on the main.dart file, which is under the "lib" folder. The source code will be stored under this "lib" folder. As you can see in our main.dart file from the image above, it contains the main function we discussed in the previous chapter. The current code is in the main.dart file is the default app code we get whenever we start a new Flutter project. Before we proceed, I would advise you to delete the test folder as in the book, we are not going over testing, so this folder is currently useless. You can feel free to keep it if you like. However, I would advise that you delete it. To delete this folder, just right-click on the test folder, click "delete" and click the "Delete" button that asks you to confirm your decision to delete that folder. The other files that you see are the configuration files needed for our app. But right now, you don't need to worry about those. As you scroll through the main.dart file, it may seem complicated, but in reality, all it is doing is defining classes and building out a basic widget tree with several widgets, including the Scaffold, AppBar, Text, Center, and Column widgets. Don't worry if you do not understand it just yet. We will be going over all of this together, but for now, I want to show you what this code looks like when run on an Android device. To run this app on a simulator, you first need to open up the simulator, which you can do by clicking the simulator that you want to run the app on under this simulator section.

Once you do that, the simulator should open up on your computer, and then you can click the green triangle, which represents the run button.

Once you press that button, the app will take some time to load, and you will see it on your simulator screen. Once it shows up on your simulator screen, it should look something like this:

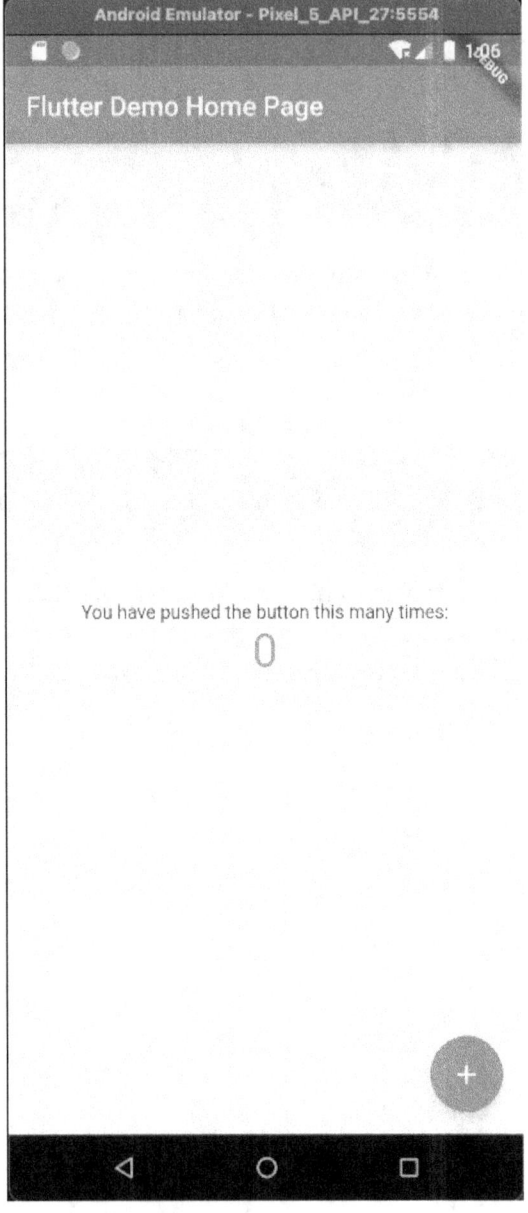

As you can see, most of the widgets used in the main.dart file was pretty self-explanatory; you have the text, the button, and its alignment in the center. The AppBar widget corresponds to the horizontal bar at the top of the simulator screen. If you press the button, then you will see that the text updates corresponding to how many times you pressed the button just as the text says. Now that we have run the app let's try to make sense of the code in the file a little more. At the top of the file, we have an import statement that is just used to import dart into our file, and then we have the main function, which, as I mentioned before, is the first function called. This main function is returning a runApp function which is running our app. The "MyApp" inside the parenthesis of the runApp function is the root widget, the parent of all widgets in the widget tree. Or in other words, the root widget is the widget that contains all the other widgets used within our app. When this widget is passed into the runApp function as a parameter, it says that the app should be run with all of the data for its appearance stored inside this MyApp widget. Below this, the MyApp widget is defined, and it extends StatelessWidget. An important thing to note is that widgets are just classes defined by using the class keyword. Don't worry if you don't understand what functions, parameters, and classes are just yet, as we will go over those in later chapters. Below the definition of the MyApp widget, you see the build function is defined, and it returns a MaterialApp widget which is a wrapper that allows us to do interface designing inside it, such as the title of the app. At the bottom of the scope of this widget, you see a line with the text "home" on it. This line defines what widget should be loaded on our home screen. In that line, we say that the "MyHomePage" widget should be loaded onto our home screen, and we also pass in a title in that line. Later in the file, we see the MyHomePage widget being defined, and if you scroll down, you will see another build function that, this time, returns our widget tree. This widget tree, as I mentioned above, contains several widgets. Some of the things inside this build function are the scaffold widget (which provides a basic structure to the interface of our app), the appBar widget (which is the blue bar you see on the top of the simulator), the text widget for the appBar, the body property which is where the content of the screen is defined, a center widget to put everything in the center, a column widget to add columns to the screen, and a floating action button widget which is the blue button you see in the bottom right corner of the simulator. This may seem very complicated, so to make it much easier, we are going to start from scratch. To do this, delete all the code inside the main.dart file and just type the following code:

```
import 'package:flutter/material.dart';

void main() => runApp();
```

Once you have typed that code, if you try and run the app, it won't work because we are not actually passing in a root widget into the runApp function. In order to fix this, we need a root widget. We could create our own root widget like the starting code in the main.dart file did, but seeing as some of you may not understand the concepts of classes and stateful widgets and stateless widgets, we are going to avoid doing that for now. Instead, we are going to pass in the MaterialApp widget and this allows us to create a blank app and acts as a wrapper for the rest of our widgets. Once you pass it in, your main function should look like this:

```dart
void main() => runApp(MaterialApp());
```

At the moment, if you run this app, all you will see is a blank simulator screen like this:

Once you see this, you might be wondering why there is a blank black screen on our simulator? Well, that is because we did not add any widgets to it. So we are going to add some text inside our MaterialApp widget. In order to do this, select the parenthesis right next to the MaterialApp widget not the last one on the outside. Make sure you are in the middle of those 2 parentheses and click the enter key. Once you do that your void function should look like this.

```
void main() => runApp(MaterialApp(

));
```

You will also notice that you are automatically indented into a new line within the scope of the MaterialApp widget. When you press the enter key between the parentheses of a widget, you are expanding its scope so you can add more code for that widget. On this new line, we are going to specify the home property so we can actually change the design of our app. So, on this new line type the following:

```
home: Text("Brand new app"),
```

This line is basically adding text to our simulator screen and the reason why we add a comma at the end is that we are going to add more lines later and whenever you add a new line below an existing line, you need to have a comma on the previous line. Once you add that line and run the app, the simulator's screen should look like this:

Now that we have added text to our app's screen, let's start adding more widgets. In order to do this, we are going to delete our text widget and implement a scaffold widget that allows us to create a basic layout for our app. To add our scaffold widget, we first need to remove the text widget from the "home" property and add the scaffold widget there and expand its scope. Once you do that, your main function should look like this:

```
void main() => runApp(MaterialApp(
  home: Scaffold(

  ),
));
```

Now that we have added our scaffold widget, let's add an app bar. If you remember how to define an app bar, go ahead and try to implement it. However, if you don't remember how to implement it, remember the basic pattern of the widget tree. In the widget tree, you have a widget that has several properties (which is why we expand its scope) and some of these properties could also be widgets that have several properties of their own and so on and so forth. This nested widget structure makes up the widget tree. So in order to create an app bar, we first need to specify the app bar widget and then specify some of its properties such as its text. Furthermore, we can also add the "centerTitle" property which is a boolean (true or false) that allows us to center our text within the app bar. Once we implement all of those, our main function should look like this:

```
void main() => runApp(MaterialApp(
  home: Scaffold(
    appBar: AppBar(
      title: Text("This is my app bar"),
      centerTitle: true
    ),
  ),
));
```

Once we do this, we will see a blue bar at the top of our simulator screen with text in the center that reads, "This is my app bar". Now that we have done that, let's add some text to our app, and we should also make this centered. Since we have already created our app bar, this text will go in the app's body, which means we need to use the "body" property. When we center text in the app's body, we can't use the centerTitle property like with the app bar. Instead, we need to use the center widget and add the text inside of that widget as a property called "child". Once you do that, your main function should look like this:

```
void main() => runApp(MaterialApp(
  home: Scaffold(
    appBar: AppBar(
      title: Text("This is my app bar"),
      centerTitle: true
    ),
    body: Center(
      child: Text("This is some text in the center")
    )
  ),
));
```

Once you have added that and you run your app, it should look something like this:

It's starting to look more like the starting app, right? However, there is still one thing that we are missing which is a button. A button allows the user to interact with the app by clicking it, and we won't be going over how to implement any functionality with the button. Instead, we are going to focus on just making the button appear. There are several button widgets, but we will use the "FloatingActionButton" widget for this example. Like the "Center" widget, this widget has a property called child which we can set to a text widget saying "click me". However, even though we are not implementing any functionality, we still need to create the function that handles the logic for when the button is pressed. For now, this function will be left blank, and don't worry about how the functions work; I will explain it in a later chapter. The code for the main function with the addition of the button is shown below:

```
void main() => runApp(MaterialApp(
  home: Scaffold(
    appBar: AppBar(
      title: Text("This is my app bar"),
      centerTitle: true
    ),
    body: Center(
      child: Text("This is some text in the center")
    ),
    floatingActionButton: FloatingActionButton(
      onPressed: () {},
      child: Text("click")
    ),
  ),
));
```

Once you write this code and run the file, then your simulator screen should look like this:

FLUTTER CODE EXPLAINED AND LEARNING OUR FIRST WIDGETS!

This is my app bar

This is some text in the center

click

You have just created your first user interface in Flutter! If you find Flutter easy, that is great to hear as you can design some beautiful-looking user interfaces with it. However, if you find Flutter rather difficult to learn, don't worry too much. It will get easier over time with practice, although I will warn you that the rest of this book will push you out of your comfort zone if you are not finding Flutter easy so far. You are now ready to start understanding stateful vs. stateless widgets and how that affects our apps.

7

Stateless and Stateful Widgets

Stateless and stateful widgets are the 2 main types of widgets in Flutter. As you may remember, a widget in Flutter is defined as a specific element on the screen of the Flutter app. Flutter code is generally written as a tree of widgets, and the appearance of the screen is entirely dependent on the choice and order of widgets used in the building of the app. Each of these types of widgets has several specific widgets under that category that can be used for various things. The difference between stateless and stateful widgets lies in whether they are changed or not. Stateless widgets do not change regardless of user interaction whereas stateful widgets do change when user interaction occurs. This also applies to their storage of data. Stateless widgets can store data however that data has to be final and be there since the widget was initialized. However, in stateful widgets, the data stored can change. An example is the starting app we see when we create a new Flutter project. The text must update every time the button is clicked, so it is a stateful widget. Furthermore, if we structure our code to use stateless and stateful widgets, we make our code more reusable and enable hot reload. Hot reload is a feature in Flutter where all you have to do is save your code base, and the simulator automatically updates instead of us having to click the run button every single time. To understand these concepts more clearly, let's break up this chapter into 2 main parts: stateless widgets and stateful widgets. In this chapter, we will also be updating our current code to incorporate these concepts.

Stateless Widgets

As previously mentioned, stateless widgets do not change regardless of user interaction. A specific widget can extend the stateless widget class meaning that they inherit their properties (which we will talk about more when we go over inheritance with classes in the next chapter). Some widgets that extend the stateless widget class and, therefore, are stateless are the following: the Text, RaisedButton, Icon, and IconButton widgets. Stateless widgets override the build function and return a widget that can be expanded into a widget tree. Speaking of that, we will now start implementing our first stateless widget. To create a stateless widget class in Flutter, you can just type "stless" and then press the tab key. Once you do that, the basic code for a stateless widget should be automatically created, and you can just type "Home" for the name of the class. The next thing we need to do is paste our existing widget tree into the return statement of this class. You can delete the code in the void function to do this, but make sure you copy it first. After that is all done, your main.dart file should look like this:

STATELESS AND STATEFUL WIDGETS

```
import 'package:flutter/material.dart';

void main() => runApp();

class Home extends StatelessWidget {

  @override
  Widget build(BuildContext context) {
    return Scaffold(
      appBar: AppBar(
          title: Text("This is my app bar"),
          centerTitle: true
      ),
      body: Center(
          child: Text("This is some text in the
          center")
      ),
      floatingActionButton: FloatingActionButton(
          onPressed: () {},
          child: Text("click")
      ),
    );
  }
}
```

If you have a line regarding keys, then just delete that line for now as we are not using it. Before we go any further, let me explain what the build function is doing. In a nutshell, the build function is responsible for building our widget tree, which is why it returns our existing widget tree with all its nested widgets. With this build function, the existing widget tree will also be added when we use this widget. Now let's test it. If you click the run button, you will notice that we get an error. This is because our main function is empty since we haven't used the "Home" widget in our main function. To fix this, we need to change the main function to the following:

```
void main() => runApp(MaterialApp(
  home: Home(),
));
```

Once we do that, we have to click the "Hot Restart" button on the bottom of the screen, which is the button on the right in this image:

Then, the app will run again, and hot reload should be enabled. We can test this by changing the text of our button from "click" to "click me". Once changed, all you have to do is save the current file, which you can do by holding down the keys "ctrl (cmd on mac)" and "s", and then the screen should update. For many people, auto-save is enabled, so you don't need to hold down any keys, and it will update automatically. Now you should understand the basics of stateless widgets and how to implement them. Before we move on to stateful widgets, it is very important to understand what the "@override" is doing. Basically, that statement means that it is modifying the original build method from the StatelessWidget class and therefore overriding it with our new widget tree. When we create a new stateless widget that extends the StatelessWidget class, we automatically inherit the build method, but we want to modify it, which is why we are adding the "@override" statement. This concept of inheritance may seem foreign to many, but don't worry because, in the next chapter, we will cover all of these class-related topics and terms together. For now, let's move on to stateful widgets.

Stateful Widgets

As mentioned above, stateful widgets change when users interact with them (or any other form of interaction occurs). Stateful widgets are especially useful when part of the user interface being designed can change dynamically according to interaction by the user. Stateful widgets can contain changing data that can be updated and seen through the app. Now that we have covered the basic concept of stateful widgets, let's create our first stateful widget. Much like the stateless widget, stateful widgets can be created in Flutter via a shortcut in which you type "stful" and then press the tab key. Feel free to title it whatever you want. However, I will be titling it "Test". If you have a line regarding keys, then just delete that line for now as we are not using it. Once you do that, your main.dart file should look like this (if you still have the stateless widget code from the previous section of this chapter):

```
import 'package:flutter/material.dart';

void main() => runApp(MaterialApp(
  home: Home(),
));
```

```
class Home extends StatelessWidget {

  @override
  Widget build(BuildContext context) {
    return Scaffold(
      appBar: AppBar(
          title: Text("This is my app bar"),
          centerTitle: true
      ),
      body: Center(
          child: Text("This is some text in the
          center")
      ),
      floatingActionButton: FloatingActionButton(
          onPressed: () {},
          child: Text("click")
      ),
    );
  }
}

class Test extends StatefulWidget {

  @override
  State<Test> createState() => _TestState();
}

class _TestState extends State<Test> {
  @override
  Widget build(BuildContext context) {
    return Container();
  }
}
```

You may notice that the stateful widget shortcut creates 2 classes instead of 1 with the stateless widget shortcut. This is because the second class, _TestState, is used to create a state for the stateful widget we just created, meaning it can store data. This is also seen through the createState function in the first stateful widget class as it returns this new _TestState. In the second class, you may notice that the build function is being overridden and is returning a widget tree similar to when we created our own stateless widget. To demonstrate the difference between stateful and stateless widgets, let's create a piece of text on our home screen that displays your age. For this example, I will use 14, but feel free to use whatever number you want. Once you do that, your "Home" class should look like this:

```
class Home extends StatelessWidget {

  @override
  Widget build(BuildContext context) {
    return Scaffold(
      appBar: AppBar(
          title: Text("This is my app bar"),
          centerTitle: true
      ),
      body: Center(
          child: Text("14")
      ),
      floatingActionButton: FloatingActionButton(
          onPressed: () {},
          child: Text("click")
      ),
    );
  }
}
```

If your code for the "Home" class looks like this, then your simulator screen should look like this:

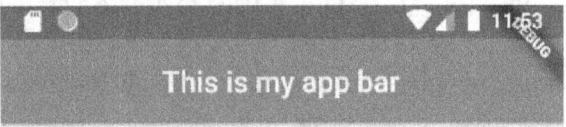

14

The only problem with this is that we can't update our age which always changes so in order to do that we need to convert the "Home" widget into a stateful widget and create an assigned variable for our age that we can update it. Firstly, we can delete our newly created stateful widget and the state class that goes along with it. Once that is done we can convert our stateless "Home" widget to a stateful widget without having to rewrite the code. All we have to do is click any letter in this line: "class Home extends StatelessWidget" and eventually a light bulb will pop up like this:

Click on that light bulb and you will see an option to convert the "Home" widget into a stateful widget. Select that option and afterward, create an integer variable called "myAge" and set it to whatever number you want. Then, your main.dart file should look like this:

```
import 'package:flutter/material.dart';

void main() => runApp(MaterialApp(
  home: Home(),
));

class Home extends StatefulWidget {

  @override
  State<Home> createState() => _HomeState();
```

```
}

class _HomeState extends State<Home> {
  int myAge = 14;

  @override
  Widget build(BuildContext context) {
    return Scaffold(
      appBar: AppBar(
          title: Text("This is my app bar"),
          centerTitle: true
      ),
      body: Center(
          child: Text("14")
      ),
      floatingActionButton: FloatingActionButton(
          onPressed: () {},
          child: Text("click")
      ),
    );
  }
}
```

Now, let's try to use this variable in our user interface. In order to do this, replace the line under the body property that says "child: Text("14")" with "child: Text("$myAge")". If you try and run the app with that code, it most likely will fail and that is because since we are adding new data we need to hot reload the app which can be done by pressing the green button on the right in this image:

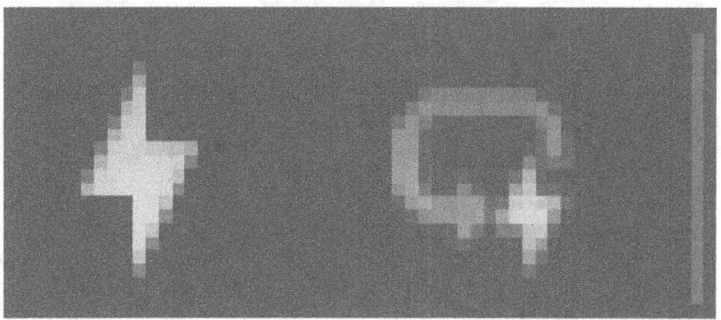

Once you click that button, the data should update. But, we want to be able to increase our age through the app. How do we achieve that? We can use the floating action button we created before to do this. Firstly, let's change the text of this button to "age up". Then we can modify the onPressed function to update our user interface when the button is clicked. To modify this function to do what we want, it is not as simple as just typing "myAge += 1" inside the function. Remember that "myAge += 1" is the same as "myAge = myAge + 1". It is just a shorthand way of typing it. The reason why it doesn't work is that it is not actually updating the state. Instead, we need to use the setState function, and inside that function, we can add our previous statement. We need to use this function because it reruns the build function with the updated data, causing the information on the screen to change. Once you do that, your main.dart file should look like this:

```
import 'package:flutter/material.dart';

void main() => runApp(MaterialApp(
  home: Home(),
));
```

```
class Home extends StatefulWidget {

  @override
  State<Home> createState() => _HomeState();
}

class _HomeState extends State<Home> {
  int myAge = 14;

  @override
  Widget build(BuildContext context) {
    return Scaffold(
      appBar: AppBar(
          title: Text("This is my app bar"),
          centerTitle: true
      ),
      body: Center(
          child: Text("$myAge")
      ),
      floatingActionButton: FloatingActionButton(
          onPressed: () {
            setState(() {
              myAge += 1;
            });
          },
          child: Text("age up")
      ),
    );
  }
}
```

Once you save the file (which is not needed if you have auto-save), then the app should work as intended, and if you press the "age up" button a few times, your screen should display the updated number like this:

STATELESS AND STATEFUL WIDGETS

This is my app bar

100

Now that you understand the difference between stateless and stateful widgets and how to implement each, you are ready to start learning more about classes and functions.

8

What are Classes and Functions in Dart?

Now that you understand the basic concept of widgets and their implementations, you may be confused by all the new terms introduced to you, such as classes, inheritance, functions, parameters, etc. In this chapter, we will be going over functions and classes, and once you understand these concepts, you will understand all of the terms above. To make this chapter less cluttered, it will be split into 2 sections: functions and classes.

Functions

Functions are very important in programming as they greatly improve code usability and readability. To understand why functions are important, you must first understand algorithms. An algorithm is a sequence of steps taken to solve a particular problem. For example, figuring out if you are a teenager, child, or an adult given your age. This algorithm would look something like this:

```
myAge = 14;
if (myAge >= 18) {
    print("You are an adult");
} else if (myAge >= 13 && myAge < 18) {
    print("You are a teenager");
} else {
   print("You are a kid");
}
```

As you can see, the problem that is algorithm is solving is determining whether you are a teenager, an adult, or a child. This problem is solved by following the sequence of steps in this algorithm through several conditionals. Imagine if there were several places in our code where we needed to determine if our user was an adult, a teenager, or a child. Then, we would need to type this algorithm every single time because the myAge variable could be different in different parts of the code, and this only returns the desired output in that portion of the code. Typing this algorithm several times can be extremely annoying and greatly increase our code's length. While the length of the code base is not directly proportionate to lack of readability, the amount of repeated code is. For this reason, we use functions. With functions, we have a place to store our algorithm that can be called anywhere in the code. Functions have return values and parameters, which we will learn briefly. But we could also use a function if we just wanted to output several print statements. An example of a function like this is shown below:

```
void printStatements() {
    print("This");
    print("is");
    print("a");
```

```
    print("very");
    print("very");
    print("long");
    print("sentence");
}
```

The above function can be used anywhere in our code, but remember that it needs to be called in our main function unless it is being called in another function (which would then need to be called in the main function). Functions are different from variables in that they can be type-specific but can't be type-inferred. Furthermore, the type definition for functions is based on that function's return value, not on the type of data stored with variables. So what are return values? The best way to understand this is as a different way of printing something within a function. Although it's not exactly that because once you return a value from a function, the code below that function is no longer executed, and in fact, most programming languages have error messages in place to prevent you from typing after a return statement. Return statements can also be used like a break statement which just breaks out of the current scope. Keep in mind that if you used a return statement in an if condition, it only returns a value and breaks out of the function, assuming that the if condition is true. Otherwise, the rest of the code will be executed until it reaches another return statement, if there is one. In the above function, we specified it as a void return type function because we were not going to return anything since we were printing everything in our function. You might be asking, what is the point of returning if we can just print everything? Well, firstly, if you have a function that prints everything, then you can't print it because then you are just printing print statements. Secondly, if you return a value in a function, you can store the result in a variable for future use. If you printed a function like the one we have above, then you would get a result like this:

```
main.dart:2:9: Error: This expression has type 'void' and can't be used.
  print(printStatements());
```

However, if you defined a function called nums that returned an integer, and if it returned 5, you could print that function because all the console would output is the return value which is 5. The function would look like this:

```
int nums() {
   return 5;
}
```

And if you printed this function, the console would just output the return value which is 5. Keep in mind that since we specified that this function was going to return an integer, if we return a string or a boolean or any other data type, then the code wouldn't run, and you would get an error like this:

```
> dart main.dart
main.dart:10:10: Error: A value
of type 'String' can't be return
ed from a function with return t
ype 'int'.
  return "5";
         ^

exit status 254
>
```

If you are wondering how to print the output of a function, then you first need to understand how to call a function. To call a function, you just type its name followed by a set of parenthesis and a semicolon. This is called a function call and would have to be in the main function or in another function that is called in the main function. A function call for the nums function would look like "nums();".

Now let's build your first function. Build a function that adds 2 given numbers and returns that value so it can be printed to the console outside of the function. You may have found a way to do this by just adding 2 random numbers that you came up with inside the function, or you might have created 2 external variables outside the function and assigned a random number that you thought of to each of them. Both of these ways work but are not the most efficient way to complete this task.

So what is the most efficient way to create an "add" function like this? Well, this is when parameters and arguments come into play. Parameters are values that the function takes in to use within the code. Since the function takes in these values, they would need to be provided by the user. These values would most likely be given through their interaction with elements in our app. For now, let's assume that we know the numbers but we only want to call the "add" function using 1 line of code. This means that we wouldn't be allowed to create any other variables. In order to do this, we define our function so that it comes with 2 variables already. These variables are parameters and as of now, they have no value assigned to them. A good habit for creating parameters is to specify their type just to avoid any potential issues. Parameters work the same as normal variables because the same operations that could be done with normal variables can also be done with parameters. So in the case of this "add" function, we can simply return the sum of these 2 parameters. Keep in mind that for this to work, they both have to be of the same type, which in this case would be an integer because the return type of our function is an integer. The function would look like this:

```
int add(int num1, int num2) {
   return num1 + num2;
}
```

As you can see, since there are multiple parameters, each of them is separated by a comma, and each parameter has its own type definition. Once this function has been created, we can call it. When calling a function that contains parameters, arguments being coming into play. Arguments are the specific values that are assigned to the parameters when the function is called. When calling this function, each parameter needs to be assigned a value, and the order is important. While the order in this function might not be crucial, if we were subtracting instead, the order of the arguments would be crucial to getting the desired result. The call for this function and printing its value should look like this:

```
print(add(1, 2));
```

This format is the same for all functions. Something to note is that previously declared variables can also be used as arguments for this function. Now that we have covered all the important details about functions such as parameters, arguments, return types, and function calls, we can move on to classes and how they set the foundation for the different widgets in Flutter.

Classes

In a previous chapter, we talked about how widgets are classes but never really covered what classes are or what they mean, but I promised that we would cover them eventually. However, this is a very basic explanation of classes, as this can easily become a topic that can be written into a book by itself.

To start off, we need to answer the question of what classes are in the first place. The easiest way to understand classes is to view a class as a user-created data type (as opposed to normal data types like int, string, etc.). Classes are blueprints for objects and allow for many advantages in things like code simplification, among others. Objects are created from classes and have properties just like an object in real life would. Objects have properties that are defined by their class. An example of this is shown below in the following image from Wikipedia Commons:

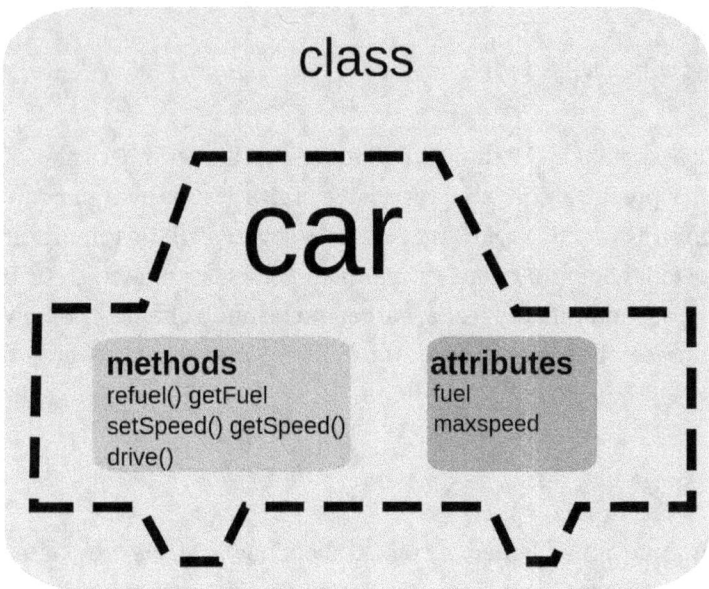

As you can see, this car class defines a set number of attributes that any object created from this class would have. An example of objects created from a class is shown in the following image from "Webcourses.ucf":

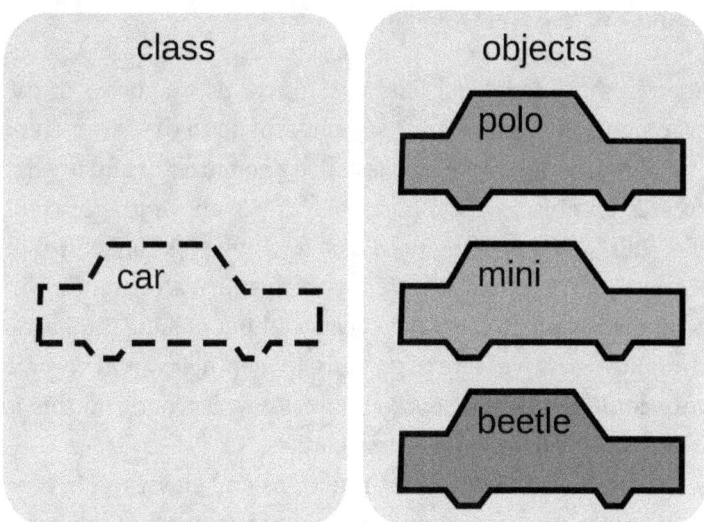

All these objects are created out of the scope of the class and have the properties fuel and maxSpeed. This class written in Dart would look like this (including only the attributes):

```
class Car {
  int fuel;
  int maxSpeed;
}
```

An important thing to consider is that in the following line of code, the variable "a" is not an object:

```
int a = 5;
```

It is not an object because an object needs to have a constructor which would look something like this (for the car example where "fuel" = 5 and "maxSpeed" = 150):

```
Car c1 = new Car(5, 150);
```

Keep in mind that, just like with functions, the order of the arguments does matter as they correspond to the parameters. The part after the equal sign is called a constructor and is what creates an object. As you can see in the above line of code, the "Car" class is being used as a data type just like "int" or "String" or others would. This is pretty much all that needs to be known about classes and objects without making things too complicated. If we were to go more in-depth, it would become very confusing and discourage most new learners, so this is where we will end off regarding classes.

Now that we have covered functions and classes, it is time to dive into a very important concept in programming: error handling.

9

Understanding and Implementing Error Handling!

Error handling is an essential component of programming as it is a fundamental part of maintaining a good user experience and makes debugging much easier.

Imagine that something in your app's code goes wrong and causes the code to stop working on a specific feature. Without error handling, what would most likely happen is that the app would crash entirely, making the user experience worse. However, with error handling, an error message can be shown on the screen saying something like, "Something went wrong, please try again later," and its design can be greatly customized. If that message looks familiar, it's because it is seen on many apps, showcasing the widespread use of error handling.

Error handling can also assist with debugging the error as it is commonly used to print the error to the console. With the error in the console, it becomes much more apparent as to what the exact error is, making it easier to fix.

There are various forms of error handling, the 2 most notable being the "try-catch" method and the "conditional" method.

In Flutter specifically, the "on-error" method involves using functions of type Future. This relates to asynchronous functions (as well as the async and await keywords), which are a more complex topic to learn. For that reason, it is not covered in this book. Both of these methods work, and at the end of the day, it comes down to personal preference when choosing what method to use. Most error handling occurs when working with databases (a separate place where data from your app is stored) or APIs (short for application programming interface where data is retrieved from another source). However, we are not working with those topics in this book. Therefore, we can try and simulate the benefit of error handling with our old code from chapter 7.

If you do not remember, this was the code for the main.dart file:

```
import 'package:flutter/material.dart';



void main() {
  runApp(MaterialApp(
    home: Home(),
  ));
}

class Home extends StatefulWidget {

  @override
  State<Home> createState() => _HomeState();
}

class _HomeState extends State<Home> {
```

```
  int myAge = 14;
  @override
  Widget build(BuildContext context) {
    return Scaffold(
      appBar: AppBar(
          title: Text("This is my app bar"),
          centerTitle: true
      ),
      body: Center(
          child: Text("$myAge")
      ),
      floatingActionButton: FloatingActionButton(
          onPressed: () {
            setState(() {
              myAge += 1;
            });
          },
          child: Text("age up")
      ),
    );
  }
}
```

Furthermore, when you run the app on an emulator, the app looks like this:

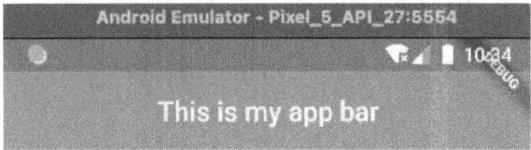

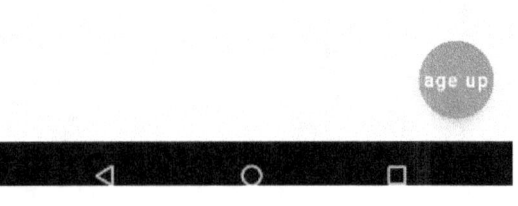

In order to simulate the "conditional" form of error handling, let's set the value of the "myAge" variable to null. One way we can do this is by the following line of code:

```
dynamic myAge;
```

When declaring the variable in this way, the value is automatically set to null. You might think that this would be the same as setting the variable to zero, but it isn't. When the value is null, the "age up" button doesn't work like it would if it was zero. When the value is null, the screen looks like this:

No matter how many times you click the button, the screen looks the same. We can fix this by adding a conditional to check if the variable's value is null. If that condition is true, then we can set it to zero. This way, our app will regain its functionality.

This might seem pointless, but imagine if we had an extremely complex app and this was a variable value returned from a function. If that value was null, we could just add a simple conditional instead of spending a lot of time debugging and ensuring that we always get a non-null value. This is a very bare-bones version of error handling that some might not even consider error handling. However, error handling prevents an error that stops our app from working. It is very simple to implement this conditional. To implement this, we just need to add an if statement that checks if the value of myAge is num, and if it is, we set myAge to zero. This condition would go in the onPressed function in the widget tree. The new _HomeState class with the widget tree should look like this:

```
class _HomeState extends State<Home> {
  dynamic myAge;
  @override
  Widget build(BuildContext context) {
    return Scaffold(
      appBar: AppBar(
          title: Text("This is my app bar"),
          centerTitle: true
      ),
      body: Center(
          child: Text("$myAge")
      ),
      floatingActionButton: FloatingActionButton(
          onPressed: () {
```

```
          if (myAge == null) {
            myAge = 0;
          }
          setState(() {
            myAge += 1;
          });
        },
        child: Text("age up")
      ),
    );
  }
}
```

Once you run the app, it should look like this:

UNDERSTANDING AND IMPLEMENTING ERROR HANDLING!

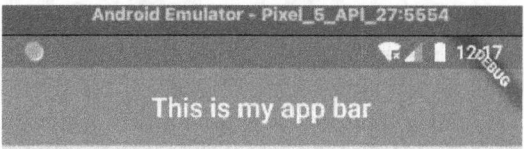

null

This looks exactly like the previous picture of the emulator screen, and that's because it is. However, if you press the "age up" button, you will notice that the number starts increasing (starting at 1). This makes sense because we told the computer that when the myAge is null, myAge is equal to zero. This is a very simple example of the conditional method of error handling. It might seem simple, but it could become complex with several "if" and "else if" statements. Now that we have covered the basics of the "conditional" error handling method, we can move on to the "try-catch" error handling method.

The "try-catch" method of error handling involves a "try" and a "catch" block. The term block refers to a block (a few lines) of code within their respective scopes. The "try" block is where all the code that is trying to be executed is put, and it has the possibility to throw an exception. An exception is an invalid input that disrupts the flow of a program. The catch block is where any thrown exception can be handled without causing the app to crash. To simulate this, we need to create a function that returns an exception. Many functions built into libraries throw exceptions in the case of invalid input. Knowing how to catch exceptions and handle them is a very important skill.

Firstly we need to create a function with an integer parameter called age. This would increase the age when the button is clicked. We can also add a condition requiring the age variable to be greater than or equal to zero. This makes sense because you can't be younger than zero years older. If the age is less than zero, we can throw an exception saying, "You can't be less than zero years old". The syntax for this function would look like this:

```
void increaseAge(int age) {
  if (age >= 0) {
    setState(() {
      age += 1;
    });
  } else {
    throw new Exception("You can't be less than zero
    years old.");
  }
}
```

The setState call is essential here because when we need to reset the appearance of the "Text" widget, we need to call setState. If you remember, this was already in the onPressed method for the button. We can remove that since we already have it in our new function. For this example, I declared the variable myAge as follows:

```
int myAge = -1;
```

Next, we need to call this function in our widget tree. Specifically, this function will get called in the onPressed function for the button. Your _HomeState class with the widget tree should look something like this:

```
class _HomeState extends State<Home> {
  int myAge = -1;
  void increaseAge(int age) {
    if (age >= 0) {
      setState(() {
        age += 1;
      });
```

```dart
    } else {
      throw new Exception("You can't be less than
      zero years old.");
    }
  }
  @override
  Widget build(BuildContext context) {
    return Scaffold(
      appBar: AppBar(
          title: Text("This is my app bar"),
          centerTitle: true
      ),
      body: Center(
          child: Text("$myAge")
      ),
      floatingActionButton: FloatingActionButton(
          onPressed: () {
            increaseAge(myAge);
          },
          child: Text("age up")
      ),
    );
  }
}
class _HomeState extends State<Home> {
  int myAge = -1;
  void increaseAge(int age) {
    if (age >= 0) {
      setState(() {
        age += 1;
      });
    } else {
      throw new Exception("You can't be less than
      zero years old.");
    }
  }
  @override
```

UNDERSTANDING AND IMPLEMENTING ERROR HANDLING!

```
Widget build(BuildContext context) {
  return Scaffold(
    appBar: AppBar(
        title: Text("This is my app bar"),
        centerTitle: true
    ),
    body: Center(
        child: Text("$myAge")
    ),
    floatingActionButton: FloatingActionButton(
        onPressed: () {
          increaseAge(myAge);
        },
        child: Text("age up")
    ),
  );
}
}
```

When you run the app, the emulator screen should look like this:

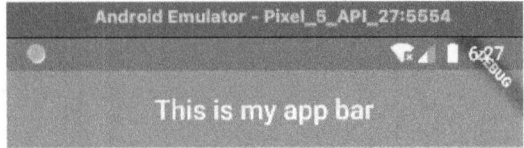

-1

This looks like the same app that we had built before. However, when you press the "age up" button, the age doesn't increase. Instead, if you look at the console in Android Studio, you should see a message like this:

```
======== Exception caught by gesture ========================================
The following _Exception was thrown while handling a gesture:
Exception: You can't be less than zero years old.

When the exception was thrown, this was the stack:
#0      _HomeState.increaseAge (package:ch_pro_tire/main.dart:25:7)
#1      _HomeState.build.<anonymous closure> (package:ch_pro_tire/main.dart:48:13)
#2      _InkResponseState._handleTap (package:flutter/src/material/ink_well.dart:1005:21)
#3      GestureRecognizer.invokeCallback (package:flutter/src/gestures/recognizer.dart:198:24)
#4      TapGestureRecognizer.handleTapUp (package:flutter/src/gestures/tap.dart:613:11)
#5      BaseTapGestureRecognizer._checkUp (package:flutter/src/gestures/tap.dart:298:5)
#6      BaseTapGestureRecognizer.handlePrimaryPointer (package:flutter/src/gestures/tap.dart:232:7)
#7      PrimaryPointerGestureRecognizer.handleEvent (package:flutter/src/gestures/recognizer.dart:563:9)
```

Imagine if there was a bug like this in our app. The app would just stop working, and our app would not receive good feedback from users. Furthermore, the exception's message is clear because we defined it. Sometimes, the exception's message is unclear regarding what needs to be fixed. We can implement a "try" block and a "catch" block to fix this.

Creating a custom error message to display this error to the user is much easier because we have already caught the error. The only issue with displaying an error message to the user is that it involves a lot of design because the alert needs to be designed. Seeing as this is a bare-bones example, we will print a message to the console. Later down the line, we can create a custom alert that can display messages to the user.

We will add this "try" block and "catch" block in the "on-Pressed" function for the button. Once we do that, the "_Home-State" class with the widget tree should look like this:

```dart
class _HomeState extends State<Home> {
  int myAge = -1;
  void increaseAge(int age) {
    if (age >= 0) {
      setState(() {
        age += 1;
      });
    } else {
      throw new Exception("You can't be less than
      zero years old.");
    }
  }
  @override
  Widget build(BuildContext context) {
    return Scaffold(
      appBar: AppBar(
          title: Text("This is my app bar"),
          centerTitle: true
      ),
      body: Center(
          child: Text("$myAge")
      ),
      floatingActionButton: FloatingActionButton(
          onPressed: () {
            try {
              increaseAge(myAge);
            } catch (e) {
              print("Invalid input for age variable");
            }
          },
          child: Text("age up")
      ),
    );
  }
}
```

The app looks exactly the same if we run it. However, if we

click the button, we get a different result in the Android Studio console. Your Android Studio console should look like this:

```
I/flutter (13635): Invalid input for age variable
```

At this point, we have covered both of the most common error handling methods: the "conditional" method and the "try-catch" method. Now that we have done this, we have learned everything necessary to create an app. In the next chapter, we will complete learning about Flutter development by publishing our current app to the public.

10

Let's Deploy Our App to the Public!

Throughout this book, you have learned the necessary skills to create a basic Flutter app. However, how do you release your app to the public? Unfortunately, for both the Google Play Store and the Apple App Store, a fee must be paid to publish apps. Although this might mean that you can't publish any app right now, it doesn't mean that you will never be able to. In this chapter, you will learn how to export your app into a format that can easily be uploaded to the Google Play Store. We will not be covering the steps for the App Store in this chapter because it requires that you have a Mac with Xcode. There are other ways to publish it on the App Store without a Mac. However, it can become really complicated. The app in question will be the "Age Up" app that we built in chapter 7. If you wish to include the code about error handling covered in the previous chapter, feel free to do so. However it doesn't make a difference because we simulated the error ourselves. Firstly, we need to set the "myAge" variable to equal zero so that the app actually works.

Publishing On the Google Play Store

The first thing that we need to do is get an image for our app icon. You can use any free image you would like. Then, search "Android icon generator" in a browser and click the first link. That link should lead to a website that looks like this:

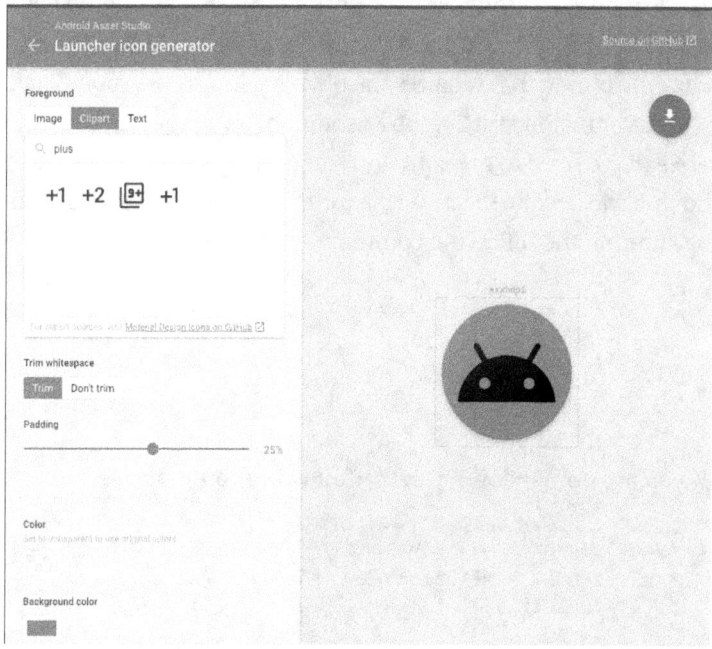

If you can't find an image, you can also use the clip art section to find basic elements to create your icon. Feel free to play around with the settings, but don't change the "Name" field at the bottom of the page. When you are satisfied with the icon, click the download button at the top right of the page.

Once you have downloaded the icon files, you need to open 2

windows of your operating system's file app (finder for mac, file explorer for Windows, or whatever file app you have installed on your computer). In the first window, open the "res" folder from the icon folder that you just downloaded so that you can see all the files. In the second window, open the path AndroidStudioPr ojects/[your project name]/android/app/src/main/ res. Expand that "res" folder and drag all the files from the first window (under the "res" folder) to the second folder. You should get a prompt telling you that there are duplicate files. For this prompt, click the option that replaces the old file with the new one. Then, you have finished setting up the icon for your app.

Next, we need to give our app a digital signature. In order to do this, we need to create a keystore for our app. We can do this by running the following command on Mac/Linux:

```
keytool -genkey -v -keystore ~/upload-keystore.jks
-keyalg RSA -keysize 2048 -validity 10000 -alias
upload
```

If you are on Windows, run the following command:

```
keytool -genkey -v -keystore
c:\Users\USER_NAME\upload-keystore.jks -storetype JKS
-keyalg RSA -keysize 2048 -validity 10000 -alias
upload
```

If you get an error when you run the command, then you should try reinstalling the Java JDK, which you can do by typing "install Java JDK" into a search engine and clicking on the first link (it should lead to a page on oracle.com). When you run the above command, make sure to remember to keep track of the passwords you enter. Furthermore, if you don't want to answer any personal questions that are asked when you run the command, you can just press the enter key. Finally, when you are prompted to confirm your information, type "yes" and keep the terminal window open.

In Android Studio, we need to create a new file called key.properties under the android section. To do this, right-click on the android file and select the new file option like shown in the image below:

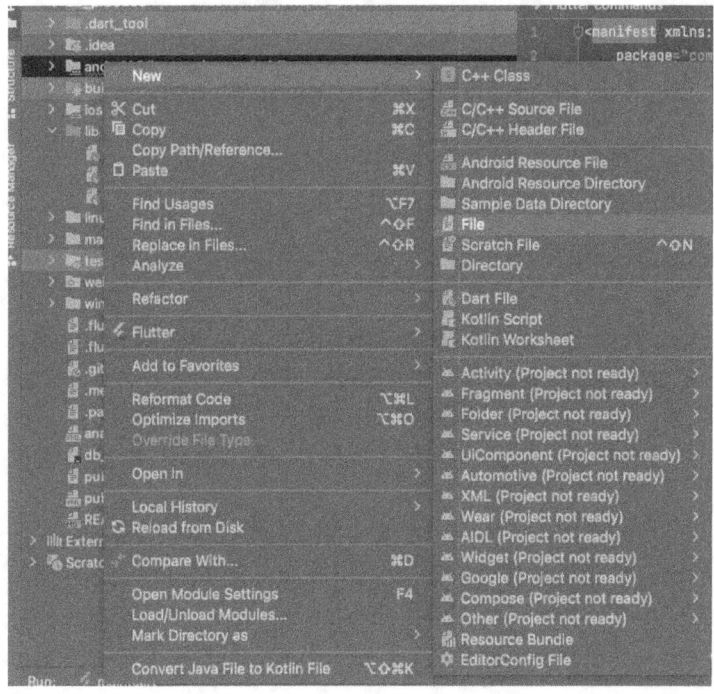

Once that file is created, add the following lines inside of the file (no need to use quotation marks):

```
storePassword= [password chosen when command was run]
keyPassword= [password chosen when command was run]
keyAlias=upload
storeFile= [location at the bottom of the terminal
window; should say Storing:____]
```

Then, open build.gradle in the app folder (inside of the android folder) and add the following lines before the line of code that reads "android {". Add these following lines of code before that line:

```
def keystoreProperties = new Properties()
def keystorePropertiesFile =
rootProject.file('key.properties')
if (keystorePropertiesFile.exists()) {
    keystoreProperties.load(new
    FileInputStream(keystorePropertiesFile))
    }
```

Next, scroll down to the line that says "minSdkVersion" and change it so that it looks like this:

```
minSdkVersion 19
```

After that, scroll down to the line that says "signingConfig signingConfigs.debug" and change it to "signingConfig signingConfigs.release". Above the line that reads "buildTypes {", add the following code:

```
signingConfigs {
   release {
       keyAlias keystoreProperties['keyAlias']
       keyPassword keystoreProperties['keyPassword']
       storeFile keystoreProperties['storeFile'] ?
       file(keystoreProperties['storeFile']) : null
       storePassword
       keystoreProperties['storePassword']
   }
}
```

Make sure to fix any indentation errors as well. Next, in the terminal in Android Studio or in the terminal app (make sure it is rooted in the project directory), run the following command:

```
flutter clean
```

After this, open AndroidManifest.xml, which can be found by the path: /android/app/src/main/AndroidManifest.xml. If you don't understand how to read paths like this, just open all the folders in order from left to right. The last term is our file name. In AndroidManifest.xml, change the following line of code:

```
android:label="[your project name]"
```

Change the text inside the quotation marks to whatever you want the app to be called. I am calling the app "Age Up". After this, there is only one more step. Open a new terminal window and go to the root of the project directory. Then run the following command:

```
flutter build appbundle
```

If it fails, run the command "flutter clean". Also, make sure there are no minor mistakes in your key.properties file, and there are no quotation marks. If it runs successfully, you will get a path in the console output which points to a file in the build folder.

Now that we have successfully exported our app, the next step is to publish it. This is where you will have to go on your own because you have to pay to publish an app. However, it is pretty simple to do. Go to the following website:

```
https://play.google.com/console/about/
```

Click on the 3 vertical lines icon on the top left of the screen. Then you will see a menu that looks like this:

LET'S DEPLOY OUR APP TO THE PUBLIC!

Features >

Resources >

Community spotlight

Policy Center

Latest news

Go to Play Console

Click the blue button on the bottom and sign in with your Google account, and from there, you will need to create your account and pay. After that, it will be pretty simple to publish your app. This is all you need to do in order to publish a Flutter app on the Google Play Store.

11

Conclusion

At this point, you are equipped with all the knowledge to start pursuing Flutter in much more detail. Enjoy the thrill of problem-solving and never give up because there is always a way to make something work! Good luck, and have fun on your development journey!

Glossary

Back-end - The place where the background logic is stored. The background logic includes things like transactions, account creation, and so on. The back-end relates to any logic not shown in the front-end.

Framework - A platform for developing applications (ex. Flutter).

Front-end - The appearance of a platform (what the user sees).

Cross-platform - The framework (or software) in question is able to run on several different devices (sometimes with different operating systems).

Native development - Development only for a specific operating system.

Console - The area (usually in an IDE) where output from an application is shown (including errors, print statements, etc).

Widgets - T components of the user interface in Flutter.

Stateless Widget - Widgets that do not change regardless of user interaction.

Stateful Widget - Widgets that can change with user interaction.

Function - A reusable section of code that can be called in various places without having to repeat the same code multiple times.

Parameter - A variable that is only allowed to be used in the function that it is referenced in.

Argument - A value that is passed in place of a parameter when the function is called.

Class - A blueprint for creating objects (includes methods and values that the objects have).

Object - An object is created from a class and has properties that were given to it by the class it was defined from.

Object-Oriented Programming Language - A programming language that is based around classes and objects (ex. Dart).

About the Author

Kaushik Madapati is a 15-year-old programmer who has enjoyed coding since he was young. He has published several apps to the Apple App Store and the Google Play Store. Furthermore, he has received several awards for his apps from the 39th Congressional district of California across several years.

Kaushik has experience in iOS, Android, and blockchain development and is currently a sophomore in high school. Since the publishing of this book, he has furthered his development journey by partaking in competitive programming and continuing to build and publish apps. He hopes to inspire younger developers like him to take bold steps and to ignore assumptions placed on them in regards to their development skill. Further information about him can be found at the links below:

Email: madapatikaushik@gmail.com

You can connect with me on:
  🔗 https://www.linkedin.com/in/kaushik-madapati-57533a1a3

www.ingramcontent.com/pod-product-compliance
Lightning Source LLC
Chambersburg PA
CBHW071418210526
45465CB00001B/441